Am I Trusting?

Written and Illustrated by

Jeannie St. John Taylor

KREGEL Kidzone

STINKY PIG SLOP

Am I Trusting?

© 2004 by Jeannie St. John Taylor

Published by Kregel Kidzone, an imprint of Kregel Publications, P.O. Box 2607, Grand Rapids, Michigan 49501.

ISBN 0-8254-3721-0

Printed in China

04 05 06 07 08 / 5 4 3 2 1

To Jodi Kinzinger—
my sister, my friend.

I walk into my house after school and see Aunt Laurel waiting for me. She says Dad took Mom to the hospital, so I have to stay at the farm with her and Cousin Sloan for a few days. My heart pounds so hard, I can hear it. I close my eyes and pray, "God, I'm scared. Please help me trust you."

We drive up the lane to her house, and I lift my bag out of the car. The hugest dog I've ever seen rushes at me, barking and showing his teeth. I drop my suitcase and throw both arms around Aunt Laurel's legs. I'm shaking all over, but I tell myself that I know God will protect me. Am I trusting God when I think that? Even if I'm not sure it's true?

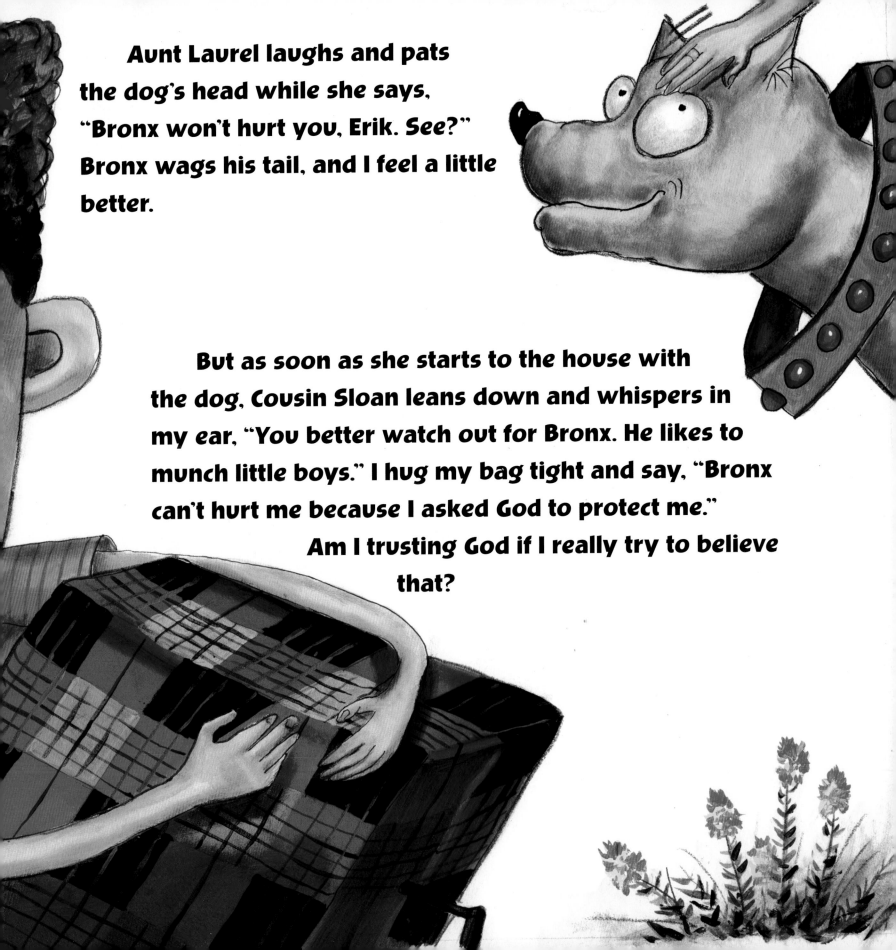

Aunt Laurel laughs and pats the dog's head while she says, "Bronx won't hurt you, Erik. See?" Bronx wags his tail, and I feel a little better.

But as soon as she starts to the house with the dog, Cousin Sloan leans down and whispers in my ear, "You better watch out for Bronx. He likes to munch little boys." I hug my bag tight and say, "Bronx can't hurt me because I asked God to protect me."

Am I trusting God if I really try to believe that?

Cousin Sloan leads me up to his room and points at the top bunk. "That's where you sleep," he says. Halfway up the ladder, I look down. It's higher than a mountain, but I hang on and whisper, "I know God won't let me fall out of bed in the middle of the night. I won't be afraid." Then I think, "I bet God gave me the top bunk so Bronx can't munch me." Is that trusting God?

The next morning Cousin Sloan and I play at the creek. He leaps from rock to rock across the water, then calls out, "Come on—you can do it." I want my cousin to like me, so I try my best, but I splash into the water and get my boots wet.

"Uh-oh," says Cousin Sloan. He squints his eyes at me and warns in a scary voice, "When kids ruin their shoes, Mom makes them visit Old Hopkins, the pig farmer. That's worse than having Bronx munch you."

I tiptoe into the house, but Aunt Laurel sees me anyway. She says, "Leave your shoes by the door to dry, then change into some clean pants so I can mend that pocket."

She doesn't say anything about Old Hopkins, so I feel happy. While I skip upstairs to change clothes, I thank Jesus for protecting me from the pig farmer. I decide I'm getting pretty good at trusting. But when I come back downstairs and hand my torn pants to Aunt Laurel, she says, "Have you ever slopped pigs, Erik?"

She smiles like she is giving me a birthday present. "I'm taking you to visit Mr. Hopkins the pig farmer today."

I feel my eyes grow big with fear.

Cousin Sloan leans close and whispers into my ear, "I told you so."

I close my eyes and beg God to help me. I tell him I know he won't let harm come to me. Am I trusting God when I tell him that? Even if I'm more scared than I've ever been in my whole life?

At the pig farm, Mr. Hopkins waits on his tractor with the motor running. He grins and waves when we drive up. He must really enjoy punishing little boys.

"Hop up on the back with the slop buckets," he says to me. I hold onto the side of the trailer and climb up really slow. I tell myself I don't have to be afraid, because God is with me. I'm surprised when Cousin Sloan springs up onto the trailer beside me.

Mr. Hopkins starts the tractor and we bump across the field toward the barn. The pig slop sloshes around in the buckets. Cousin Sloan laughs and whoops above the sound of the tractor. He points at the slop. "That's the pig food," he tells me. I shudder.

The tractor stops at the barn and the pigs run over, squealing for food. The baby ones look cute, but I'm too busy trusting God to really notice.

When we get to the pigpen, Cousin Sloan is laughing so hard he has to lean against the fence. "You don't have to eat pig food, Erik," he says. "I was playing a joke on you."

"A joke?" I feel confused.

"Yeah. Feeding pigs is fun."

I say, "You sure fooled me good," and we stand there in the pigpen, laughing together for the longest time.

Then we grab stinky buckets of slop from the trailer. We feed the pigs and watch them gobble up their food. It is fun. Cousin Sloan was right.

The next morning, Mom and Dad pull up to Aunt Laurel's farmhouse with another surprise for me: a brand new baby sister!

Aunt Laurel hugs me goodbye, Bronx slurps a kiss across my face, and Sloan pulls me into a headlock. "I'll sure miss you, Erik. Wanna come visit us again?"

"I sure do," I say. "This is the most fun I've ever had."

I finally understand that if you want life to turn out well, you just have to make yourself trust God.

For Parents

There is one good thing about fear—it can trigger faith. The mere fact that Erik turned to God every time something bad happened revealed a seed of trust in his heart. His faith may not yet be perfect, but it will grow stronger and stronger as he deliberately practices trusting God.

Read it together

As you read the book with your child, take note of all Erik's fears. Visual clues in the illustrations will tell you if they are real or imagined.

Talking it over

Discuss which fears were real and which ones were imagined or exaggerated. Ask your child to tell you some of his or her fears. Are they real or imagined? Does he or she try to trust God when they feel afraid? Is it still trusting even if the fears aren't real? *Hint: Erik and I both think it is.*

Taking action

Direct your child to write out Proverbs 3:5–6, "Trust the Lord with all your heart. Don't depend on your own understanding. Remember the Lord in everything you do. And he will give ou success" on a 3 x 5 card. Decorate it with stickers or markers. Decide to make trusting your goal.

Just for fun

To help your child practice trust, tell them to stand with their back to you and fall backward, trusting that you'll catch them. Once they turn their back to you, remain silent so that they have no way of knowing that you are really there. See if they can fall without looking back to make sure you are really there and ready to catch them. Do this activity several times. Is it easier for them to overcome their fears and trust you the more they fall and find that you are there?